HOMELESSNESS

HOMELESSNESS

BY A. M. BUCKLEY

Content Consultant
Ellen Munley
doctoral student of political science
Graduate Center of the City University of New York

ABDO
Publishing Company

CREDITS

Published by ABDO Publishing Company, 8000 West 78th Street,
Edina, Minnesota 55439. Copyright © 2012 by Abdo Consulting
Group, Inc. International copyrights reserved in all countries.
No part of this book may be reproduced in any form without
written permission from the publisher. The Essential Library™
is a trademark and logo of ABDO Publishing Company.

Printed in the United States of America,
North Mankato, Minnesota
062011
092011

 THIS BOOK CONTAINS AT LEAST 10% RECYCLED MATERIALS.

Editor: Karen Latchana Kenney
Copy Editor: Jennifer Joline Anderson
Design and Production: Marie Tupy

Library of Congress Cataloging-in-Publication Data
Buckley, A. M., 1968-
  Homelessness / by A.M. Buckley.
    p. cm. -- (Essential issues)
  Includes bibliographical references and index.
  ISBN 978-1-61783-134-8
  1. Homelessness--United States--Juvenile literature. 2.
Homeless persons--United States--Juvenile literature. I. Title.
  HV4505.B83 2012
  362.50973--dc22

                                        2011016517

TABLE OF CONTENTS

Teen Joe Flores became homeless after his father died from cancer, but he continued going to school.

LIFE ON THE STREETS

omes are meant to provide safety, but for Joey, a young boy growing up in Mississippi, home was a place of fear. He was regularly taped to a table and beaten by his father. At age 12, Joey left his abusive home. He boarded a bus and

traveled to Washington DC, where he lived in an abandoned car.

Joey was resourceful. He found food and managed to enroll in classes at a local school. Having suffered physical and emotional abuse for years at home, he tried hard to protect himself from further violence on the streets. He avoided drug dealers, pedophiles, and other people who sometimes prey on children living alone on the streets.

Joey traveled from one place to another, living in makeshift homes. He recalled, "I stayed in baseball dugouts, abandoned warehouses, boxes sometimes. I remember staying under a bridge then too. I did okay, mostly."[1]

Joey dreamed of living in California. He continued moving, making his way west. One night, in Houston, Texas, he met some outreach workers from Covenant House, an organization dedicated to

"Each year, more than 3 million people experience homelessness, including 1.3 million children. And according to national studies, even more Americans are at risk of homelessness."[2]
—*National Law Center on Homelessness and Poverty, 2010*

From War to Homelessness

Homelessness is an issue that affects many veterans of the armed services. Sergeant Vanessa Turner served in the Iraq War for seven years. She fell ill while driving a supply truck in the desert and was in a coma for nearly a week. Doctors pronounced her case incurable, but Turner survived. When she returned home to Boston, Massachusetts, she had no place to live. Injuries from her illness prevented her from finding a job, and due to a mix-up at the veterans' hospital, her much-needed medical treatment was delayed. Homeless and without the means to find or maintain a home of her own, she stayed on a friend's couch. Turner had served her country and narrowly escaped death only to face a new struggle at home.

helping homeless children and teens. The outreach workers offered him a sandwich and juice. They talked to him about his situation and how they might be able to help.

Joey received shelter and aid from Covenant House. He took classes and graduated from high school. Eventually, he moved on once more to pursue his dream of living in California. This time, he was armed with a diploma and a network of support.

Homeless Children and Adolescents

Joey is one of many children who have been homeless. His story had a happy ending, but not all children and teens receive support like he did. In the United States every year, one in 50 children is homeless. Most live with their families at the homes of friends or relatives. Approximately 44 percent live in shelters, motels,

or on the streets. Many, like Joey, leave abusive parents. Others are left alone after single parents die. Some children have been placed in one foster home after another and, when they turn 18 and leave foster care, are left without any place to go.

Homeless children and teens struggle to find a place to sleep, food to eat, and transportation to get to school. Some drop out of school because the anxiety and frustration of homelessness make it too hard to keep up. Not knowing where they will sleep, they are constantly on the move. Without a bathroom, it is hard to stay clean. These children also suffer teasing and bullying by students who cannot comprehend the immense struggle of homelessness.

Like other homeless children, Joey struggled daily to find food and shelter. But he was fortunate to avoid dangers many homeless children and teens face. These include being

"Children without homes are twice as likely to experience hunger as other children. Two-thirds worry they won't have enough to eat. More than one-third of homeless children report being forced to skip meals. Homelessness makes children sick. Children who experience homelessness are more than twice as likely as middle class children to have moderate to severe acute and chronic health problems. Homeless children are twice as likely as other children to repeat a grade in school, to be expelled or suspended, or to drop out of high school. At the end of high school, few homeless students are proficient in reading and math—and their estimated graduation rate is below 25%."[3]
—in America's Youngest Outcasts: State Report Card on Child Homelessness *from The National Center on Family Homelessness*

sold into prostitution, initiated into gangs, being raped or abused, or becoming addicted to drugs. Many homeless children and teens have suffered from severe violence and abuse at home. Some then become victims of more violence from strangers on the street.

When Covenant House found Joey and he accepted their offer of help, he received a safe place to sleep at night, was given food to eat, and returned to school in a supportive environment. Covenant House and other organizations are dedicated to helping the homeless. But they can help only a limited number of homeless people—many more are on the streets each night.

HOMELESSNESS TODAY

Some children and adolescents live on the street or in temporary shelters, without parents or family, as Joey did for many years. But most

**Homeless
in the United States**

According to the 2009 Annual Homelessness Assessment Report (AHAR), on a single night in January 2009 in the United States, there were approximately 643,067 sheltered and unsheltered homeless people. For the entire year, from October 2008 to September 2009, approximately 1.56 million people used emergency shelter or a transitional housing program.

Day shelters provide daytime refuge for homeless families, including single mothers and their children.

homeless children and teens are not alone. Homeless families, usually headed by single mothers, have been on the rise since the 1980s and families are the fastest-growing population of homeless people in the United States today.

To be homeless means to be without the things people are used to having in a home. People who are homeless do not have access to a bed to sleep in, a kitchen to prepare food, or a place to shower or use the bathroom. Often, they do not know where their

next meal will come from or if it will be safe to eat.
Just as Joey did, they live in a series of shelters, in
cars or motels, abandoned buildings, under bridges,
or inside tunnels. They may stay for a time with
friends or family. They usually lack access to medical
care. Homeless children rarely get vaccinations,
leaving them vulnerable to disease.

ESSENTIAL NEEDS

A home can mean many things to many people.
At the most basic level, a home provides shelter
from the elements. It is a place to sleep and relax in
privacy and safety. A home is also a place to bathe, to
use the restroom, and to prepare food. Whether it
is a small apartment, a large house, or a room over a
garage, a home provides a place to store belongings,
to gather with family or friends, to rest or do
homework, make phone calls, or watch television at
the end of a long day.

People with homes tend to take the availability
of basic amenities for granted, but not having them
presents monumental and immediate logistical
problems and deeply traumatic emotional stressors.
A person without a home has no place to do the
most basic activities of day-to-day life. Personal

hygiene becomes difficult to maintain, sleeping is a challenge, and finding food is a constant struggle.

Homeless people face the challenge of seeking ways to accommodate their basic needs.

In addition, people who are homeless face social stigma. They may be labeled as lazy, mentally ill, substance abusers, or criminals. Without knowledge of homelessness, it can be easy to accept such stereotypical views. But homelessness is a complex issue that involves larger societal problems such as

Welfare Hotels

In his 1988 book about homeless families in America, *Rachel and Her Children*, author Jonathan Kozol wrote of his visits with families living in welfare hotels in New York City. Welfare hotels, which are fairly uncommon today, once provided temporary housing for homeless families. Many of these shelters were without regular heat or working plumbing. Kozol asked,

What is life like for children in this building? For many, the question may be answered briefly, as their lives will be extremely short. The infant mortality rate in [the welfare] hotel is twenty-five per thousand, over twice the national rate and higher even than the rate in New York's housing projects.[4]

Life for the children who did survive was difficult. According to Kozol,

Their front doors will give out upon a narrow corridor; their windows on a courtyard strewn with glass, or on the street, or on the wall of an adjacent wing of the hotel. . . . Many will wait for months before they are assigned to a public school. Those who do get into school may find themselves embarrassed by the stigma that attaches to the "dirty baby," as the children of the homeless are described by hospitals and sometimes perceived by their schoolteachers.[5]

unemployment and lack of affordable housing. That is why learning what it means to be homeless and who is homeless is important before judging a homeless person's situation. This issue affects the lives of children, teens, adults, and the elderly every day.

*The widespread issue of homelessness affects young and old
in countries around the world.*

In a Philadelphia almshouse, the poor could work in a shoemaker's room to earn their shelter and food.

EARLY RESPONSES TO HOMELESSNESS

istorically, American communities have worked on a local level to solve the problem of homelessness. In colonial times, citizens typically aided friends and neighbors in need by providing lodging or food. When the

amount of people in need exceeded the resources of local families, towns established what were known as poorhouses or almshouses. This housing was supported by alms, which are donations given to churches to help the poor. Various factors could lead a person to an almshouse. Similar to contemporary shelters, almshouses were compelled to serve everyone. At almshouses, the able-bodied homeless could chop wood or perform other menial jobs in exchange for food and lodging.

In his book *Homelessness*, anthropologist Kim Hopper explained that these all-purpose refuges "nursed the terminally ill, took in the chronically disabled, put up deserted children and newly arrived strangers, and punished those whose behavior fell outside the jurisdiction of penal institutions."[1]

As the United States grew, local and state governments addressed

Police Aid

During the nineteenth century, poverty was widespread. Local police officers spent much of their time on social issues, including helping to find lost children and giving out food to people in need. Police stations also set up makeshift housing in cities across the United States.

poverty in their districts. Hopper wrote that "the poor of the nineteenth century were everywhere apparent. Begging was commonplace. Rag-pickers foraged through garbage for discarded items and scrap food."[2]

Concerns arose over how to handle people who were homeless. Many cities followed the example of New York City. In 1839, New York City set up an asylum to serve the mentally ill and disabled among the homeless population. In 1850, the city constructed an almshouse.

The Dawn of Public Assistance

In the mid-nineteenth century, the federal government became involved in aiding the poor and homeless. The federal response remained relatively limited until the 1930s, when the nation was hit with a huge economic crisis called the Great Depression.

During this time, the number of people who were unemployed, poor, and homeless swelled tremendously. Local communities and police forces providing aid were stretched to the breaking point. Federal programs aimed at providing jobs and support were set into motion. For example, the Federal Transient Program provided vouchers, or

During the Great Depression, many of the homeless lived in shack communities called Hoovervilles.

coupons, that could be traded for lodging. These vouchers helped many in New York City, where large numbers were without work and homes, but were less helpful in other areas of the country.

THE NEW DEAL

Franklin Delano Roosevelt was elected the thirty-second president of the United States in 1932, at the height of the Great Depression. Approximately 13 million people were unemployed, and banks had

collapsed all over the United States, leaving many people penniless. Widespread poverty and joblessness led to a dramatic increase in the homeless population.

President Roosevelt set into motion a series of laws that created jobs and improved both job security and quality of life for average Americans. These laws are collectively called the New Deal. One of these was the Social Security Act of 1935. This act created a federal fund that gives economic security to elderly Americans who are retired from work. It has been revised and expanded many times, and continues to support Americans today.

As part of the Social Security Act, Roosevelt also created a program called Aid to Families with Dependent Children, commonly referred to as welfare. This program gives funds to families with children who are poor and often homeless.

Aid for the Elderly

When Social Security was first established, payments were made in one lump sum. The first person to receive this form of the benefit was a man named Ernest Ackerman in a payment of 17¢. In December 1939, the Social Security system changed its method of distribution to monthly payments. This method remains in place to this day. The first recipient of monthly benefits was a woman named Ida May Fuller in Vermont. Since it was established, Social Security has allowed billions of retired Americans to have enough income to remain securely housed.

These and other programs Roosevelt enacted provide aid to Americans who are poor, unemployed, or otherwise at risk of homelessness.

THE GREAT SOCIETY

Homelessness, poverty, and unemployment decreased significantly with the New Deal programs. During the 1950s, the American middle class grew larger than ever before, but approximately 20 percent of the US population was still living in poverty.

Lyndon Johnson became

President Franklin Delano Roosevelt

Franklin Delano Roosevelt (1882–1945) served four terms as president of the United States, making him the only American president to serve more than two terms in office. Roosevelt was also the only president to use a wheelchair, having lost the use of his legs due to polio at age 39. He overcame this challenge to become a commanding, resourceful, and compassionate leader during the Great Depression and also during World War II (1939–1945).

Between 1933 and 1934, Roosevelt passed the Emergency Relief Administration. This gave funding to states to relieve unemployment by creating new jobs. He also enacted two job creation programs, the Works Progress Administration and the Civilian Conservation Corps, and a program to aid struggling farmers. From 1935 to 1936, Roosevelt passed another group of laws, including the Social Security Act.

During his second term in office, Roosevelt created the United States Housing Authority, helping to ensure the safety of all forms of housing and providing funds for public housing. In 1938, he passed the Fair Labor Standards Act, which established a minimum wage for American workers.

Through his extensive social programs, Roosevelt created a new relationship between the United States and its citizens, and a new pledge that the government would support people in need.

president in 1963 and declared a
war on poverty. In building what he
called the "Great Society," President
Johnson greatly expanded Roosevelt's
programs and increased spending for
welfare and other public programs.
These programs allowed people who
were homeless, poor, unemployed,
or a combination of these to purchase
food for their families and find
decent housing. ⌐

Issues of Federal Aid

Federal aid has been a contentious political issue. Those in favor of it generally cite a societal responsibility to provide support to those in need. Those against it tend to indicate that public support creates dependency and antisocial behavior. Both sides of the debate continue today as politicians discuss the viability of social security and welfare.

Another problem with federal aid is that many needy people tend to slip through the cracks because they are not eligible for one reason or another. Examples include families who have exceeded welfare time limits and single working-age men without disability or recent employment.

The programs that President Roosevelt created as part
of the New Deal continue to assist those in need today.

Homeless people sometimes carry their belongings in shopping carts.

CONTEMPORARY HOMELESSNESS

During the 1970s and 1980s, homelessness began increasing. The cost of living was rising during this time, making it harder for the working poor and people on welfare to afford a home. Political and economic changes during the

1980s also added to the rise of homelessness across the United States. Ronald Reagan, the fortieth president of the United States, was elected in 1981 and remained in office through 1989. Reagan instituted sweeping economic reforms that included cutting budgets for all forms of public support. Welfare was particularly hard hit. In his book *The Visible Poor,* social welfare expert Joel Blau observed that the Reagan administration "altered eligibility and payment standards three times, cutting a total of $3.6 billion and eliminating 442,000 people from the national caseload."[1]

As more and more people became homeless, they became visible on the streets and sidewalks of major metropolitan areas and, less rapidly, in smaller cities and towns.

STATES ADDRESS HOMELESSNESS

As homelessness grew in American cities and towns, states provided relief in a variety of ways. The National Governors Association created a special task force to study the extent of homelessness and to identify solutions. The resulting report, released in 1983, documented widespread homelessness and recommended federal support. Individual states offered relief in varying degrees. For example,

New York and Massachusetts both voted to expand funding for low-income housing in 1983.

Various agencies within a state may also collaborate to provide relief for homeless people. Working together, they are often better able to find solutions to homelessness and ways to provide services to homeless people. In an essay for the National Coalition for the Homeless, Vicki Watson describes the trend:

As states have experienced growth in the numbers of homeless and have obtained increased

A Bittersweet Victory

In 1979, lawyer Robert Hayes found Robert Callahan ill and asleep on the streets of the Bowery area of New York City. The city did not have enough capacity to provide shelter for all who applied, so many slept on the streets. Hayes decided to take action. He filed a lawsuit against the state of New York, seeking the basic right of access to shelter for the homeless. The lawsuit marked the beginning of The National Coalition for the Homeless, cofounded by Hayes in 1981 as the Coalition for the Homeless.

The case, called *Callahan v. Carey*, was a class action lawsuit, which means that it is placed in the name of one person but represented many. The lead plaintiff was Robert Callahan; the suit was filed on behalf of all the homeless men in New York City. It was fought in the New York State Supreme Court. Hayes argued that the state constitution gave all New Yorkers a right to shelter.

In a landmark victory, the coalition and Callahan won. On December 5, 1979, the court ordered the city and state of New York to provide shelter for homeless men. Sadly, Robert Callahan did not live to hear the decision; he died a few months before the decision was passed.

funding to assist them and to prevent homelessness, they have also focused more on state-wide collaboration among various anti-homeless agencies and services, notably through state councils, task forces, and committees. [2]

ADVOCACY FOR THE HOMELESS

Individual Americans have responded in a variety of ways to the growing number of homeless people in society. Just as colonial families took in boarders or fed the hungry, many contemporary Americans have formed soup kitchens and organized drives to collect canned foods, blankets, or other necessities for the homeless. Some gather their used clothing and furniture and donate them to homeless shelters. Others make financial donations to church groups, community organizations, and other charities that support the growing homeless population.

Union of the Homeless

In 1985, as homelessness continued to increase across the country, a group of people who were homeless banded together to form a union. Within three years, the Union of the Homeless had chapters in 14 cities. They organized strikes, marches, and sleep-ins to demonstrate the size of the homeless population. They hoped to gain access to more and better quality shelter and to engage the public to seek solutions to homelessness.

*At homeless shelters, guests receive hot meals,
a bed to sleep in, and other services.*

Another way individuals have responded to homelessness is through legal advocacy. Lawyers, judges, and human rights activists focus on creating laws to assist the homeless.

In recent decades, a variety of local and community efforts developed into a national movement. In 1982, the National Coalition for the Homeless was founded in New York City and soon moved to Washington DC. Since that time, the coalition has provided resources for homeless people and built public awareness and support for the cause. Its programs and services include a voting rights campaign for homeless people; fact sheets and news about homelessness; detailed information on national, state, and local services for those who are homeless; and an inventive initiative that gives privileged people the experience of homelessness for a day in order to build public empathy.

During the 1980s, the National Coalition for the Homeless collaborated with other advocacy groups to bring attention to the issue. Through rallies that often

"The social movement to house the homeless sees homelessness as a social problem rather than a private trouble. Politics replaces charity. Food, clothing, and shelter are no longer donations to the unfortunate. Instead, in this movement, advocates see the necessities of life as a basic human right."[3]
—*Joel Blau,
author of* The Visible Poor

included tent cities, they worked to make people aware of the widespread problem of homelessness. Their activism paved the way for the first-ever federal law for homeless people, the Homeless Persons' Survival Act, later called the Stewart B. McKinney Act. The law, which provided emergency relief to homeless in the form of shelter, food, health care, and transitional housing, was passed in July 1987 with bipartisan support from both houses of Congress.

THE STEWART B. MCKINNEY ACT

The McKinney Act, named for its primary Republican supporter who passed away before it was made into law, set aside just over $1 billion in federal funds to assist the homeless. The act recognized the increased problem of homelessness in the United States and created a council to address the issue and report to the president. It also established the

Legal Aid for the Homeless

The National Law Center on Homelessness and Poverty is the legal arm of the National Coalition for Homelessness. Founded by Executive Director Maria Foscarinis, the law center split from the National Coalition in 1989 to focus specifically on legal issues affecting homelessness and homeless people. The National Law Center on Homelessness and Poverty seeks to change laws and policies with the goal of alleviating the suffering of homeless people and ultimately ending homelessness in the United States.

Federal Emergency Food and Shelter Program to distribute funds to feed and house the homeless and improve existing shelters.

The McKinney Act further required that all cities devise plans to house their local homeless. It created federal grant programs to provide funding and support for medical care, education and job training, and counseling services for the homeless.

The McKinney Act was amended in 1988, 1990, 1992, and 1994. In 1994, the most prominent addition provided increased support for homeless children to attend public school. The act ensures that homeless children have transportation to and from school and requires schools to register homeless children even if the children do not have documents normally required, such as immunization records. This amendment, known as the McKinney-Vento Act, was last

The HEARTH Act

On May 20, 2009, President Barack Obama signed the Homeless Emergency and Rapid Transition to Housing (HEARTH) Act into law. This amendment to the McKinney-Vento Homelessness Assistance Act expanded support for the homeless in rural areas, consolidated some Housing and Urban Development programs making needed funds easier to access, and increased support for resources to prevent homelessness.

reauthorized in 2002. The McKinney Act remains the single most comprehensive federal legislation to address the issue of homelessness. In spite of these legislative changes, though, homelessness is still a pervasive and growing problem in the nation.

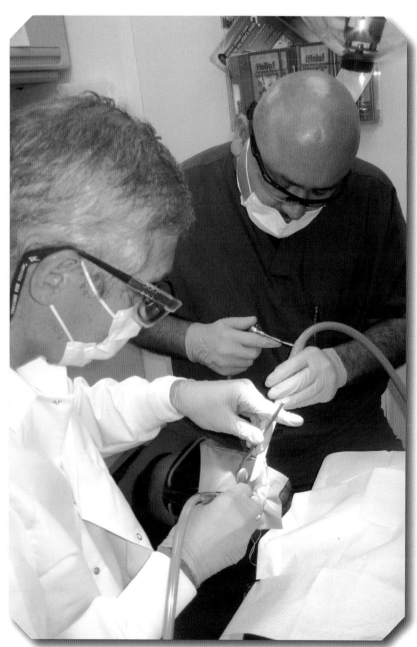

Using federal stimulus funds, dentists from a Colorado clinic offered free services to teens at a homeless teen shelter in 2009.

The public nature of homelessness
makes it a highly noticeable issue in society.

WHAT DOES IT MEAN
TO BE HOMELESS?

ost of what people accomplish in a home is considered to be private. This includes sleeping, bathing, and dressing, as well as connecting with friends and family. These important parts of life are private for those with homes, but for

homeless people the same activities must be done in the public eye. The lack of privacy is particularly difficult for homeless people to endure, as it takes away their dignity and exposes them to ridicule and judgment from the public.

In addition to the loss of privacy, a homeless person's lack of an address makes it difficult to apply for a job, get together with friends and colleagues, store and keep belongings, and feel safe. As homeless people, they find themselves disconnected from society. In his book *Reckoning with Homelessness*, Kim Hopper writes about this problem:

> To be homeless is to have suffered a fundamental rupture in the ties that bind. It signifies the breach of that intimate contract that regulates relations between private lives and the public worlds of work, consumption, political participation, and general social intercourse.[1]

As Hopper explains, and other research on homelessness confirms, people who are homeless face intense social stigma and are often blamed for their desperate situation. Hopper writes that the social response to homelessness changes with the times but includes "measures of pity and abhorrence, the impulse to care and the instinct

to avoid."[2] People with homes tend
not to understand how a homeless
person got into his or her situation.
As a result, most people have mixed
feelings toward the homeless.

Living private lives in public is also
a serious concern for safety and health.
Without a secure residence, homeless
people face threats of violence and
theft. Unsanitary living conditions and
a lack of regular meals pose big health
risks, especially when endured over
long periods of time. Even homeless
people who are able to stay in a shelter
struggle to find food and a secure space
for their belongings. The conditions
in many homeless shelters and other
temporary living spaces are inadequate
in regard to health and safety and can
be as dangerous as the streets.

What Is Homelessness?

To be homeless is to be without a
home, but there are different specific
definitions of homelessness. These

**Bread Lines
and Soup Kitchens**

People who are poor and
homeless struggle to find
adequate and nutritious
food. To meet this need,
many public, private, and
religious organizations
have worked to provide
food to the homeless. During the Great Depression,
private groups created
what were called "bread
lines" to serve food to those
in need. Commonly called
soup kitchens today, these
services are provided by a
mix of independent, reli-
gious, community-based,
and government-run
groups working at a local
level to provide food to
those who are homeless.

differences in definitions are important because federal funds are set aside for homeless services based on the number of homeless people counted. This makes the definition of homelessness affect the amount of services provided. In addition, the definition determines who is eligible to receive homeless services. The official federal government definition, outlined in the 1987 Stewart B. McKinney Act, describes a homeless person as "[a]n individual who lacks a fixed, regular, and adequate

Order and Compassion on the Street

Kim Hopper, an author and anthropologist who has studied homelessness, recounted time spent with homeless people in New York City, in the street and in shelters, during the course of his research. He noticed that despite their difficult circumstances, the people he met went to great efforts to preserve a sense of order and extend basic kindnesses to each other. Hopper saw homeless people placing blankets on sleeping companions and sharing provisions. Some risked their own safety to break up fights. These and other acts of bravery and compassion were common among the homeless Hopper met.

When Hopper appeared at shelters as a newcomer, regular inhabitants helped him by explaining rules, schedules, and where soup kitchens were located. This courtesy extended to life on the streets. Hopper recalled:

At a train station, a small group of the homeless residents was observed to come to the aid of a commuter suffering an epileptic seizure, while "respectable" passersby passed her by. Beat cops, security guards, and token-booth clerks at certain sites awakened occupants in time for work each day.[3]

A homeless person uses a park bench as a temporary "bed."

nighttime residence" or whose nighttime residence
is a temporary shelter, transitional housing for
the mentally ill, or "a public or private place not
designed for, or ordinarily used as, a regular

sleeping accommodation for human beings."[4] Examples of places not designed as sleeping accommodations include park benches, bus stops, train stations, backyards, and other spaces where people who are homeless stay for the night or for a period of time.

A broader definition of homelessness was introduced by the federal government with the 2009 HEARTH Act. It also includes people who are going to lose their housing within 14 days and families and children who are unstably housed. To be unstably housed is to not have a home and to frequently move. The new definition also includes people experiencing domestic violence who are trying to leave their homes but do not have a place to go. This definition is used to decide who is eligible for homeless assistance programs including homelessness prevention assistance.

"Americans have used the word 'homeless' in something like its modern sense for roughly 150 years. Most often, its meaning is literal and prosaic: the absence of a domicile. . . . But we also invoke the word to indicate something poignant and diffuse: the absence of belonging, both to a place and with the people settled there."[5]
—*Kim Hopper and Jim Baumohl, authors and scholars of homelessness*

Patterns of Homelessness

In measuring patterns of homelessness, advocates and scholars gather data about where homeless people live and how long they have been homeless. They must take into account not only those who are staying in homeless shelters, but also those living on the streets. Estimating how many people live on the streets is difficult, but it is necessary to create a true picture of homelessness. Whether in a shelter or on the street, people who are homeless suffer the emotional, physical, psychological, and social effects of not having a safe and sanitary place to live.

As a result of research, three different patterns of homelessness have been defined: chronic, episodic, and transitional, or temporary, homelessness. Chronic homelessness refers to a condition of being without any kind of home to call one's own for a long period of time; that is, at least one year or more than four times during the course of one year. Episodic homelessness is a condition of being homeless for multiple brief periods of time. According to the 2009 Annual Homelessness Assessment Report (AHAR), most people stay in emergency shelters for less than one week and transitional housing for less than six months. For example, seasonal workers

such as those who pick fruit or harvest crops might have homes when they have work and then be homeless during the off-season.

A third classification is called transitional homelessness, which occurs when a person or family loses a home due to a crisis. This kind of homelessness, which represents the majority of the homeless population, is usually sudden and can be caused by leaving a home because of domestic violence or losing a home due to job loss or a natural disaster. Though transitional homelessness often marks a first instance of homelessness for the affected individual or family, it can be lasting and turn into chronic or episodic homelessness.

Daily Life

Definitions of homelessness can vary, but for the person who is homeless, distinctions between

Urban Homelessness

The number of people who are homeless is on the rise around the world. Approximately 20 to 40 percent of these people live in large, urban areas. American cities, including New York, Chicago, and Los Angeles, are seeing a large increase in the numbers of homeless people. Cities in India, China, Russia, and other nations are similarly seeing more and more homeless on the streets. In Sao Paolo, Brazil, in 2009, the government worked with local community groups to find solutions to the growing homeless population. As a result, the city built housing for those who are poor and existing without shelter.

episodic or chronic and shelter or street are much less relevant. The daily reality of homelessness does not fit neatly into any single category. Simply getting basic needs met is a perpetual struggle.

There is rarely a single or simple resolution to their challenges. Most homeless people employ a variety of methods and resources to find meals, shelter, and other services. They might spend a night in a crowded shelter in order to use the shower, sleep on a park bench for a day or two, and then spend a night with a relative or friend. Combining resources is an important tool of survival for life on the streets.

"It should never be forgotten, and that's how I survive every day with as little judgment as humanly possible. I never forget that it could be me tomorrow that is living on the street, that is homeless, that has mental health issues."[6]
—*Staff member at Women Street Survivors Resource Group, a shelter for homeless women*

Many Haitians experienced transitional homelessness after a 2009 earthquake forced them to live in tents.

*A homeless fair, where people can receive free haircuts and dental checkups,
is offered in part as a way to count the homeless population.*

WHO IS HOMELESS
IN AMERICA?

Many researchers study homelessness
by focusing on the number of people
who are homeless. Methods have included counting
the numbers of homeless people living on the streets
or shelters; using telephone surveys of a sample of

the population to estimate the percentage of the population that has experienced homelessness in the last year, three years, or five years; and surveying those who work with the homeless to estimate how many people they serve. Despite these methods, scholars point out that it is very difficult to determine exactly how many people are homeless at any given time.

Researchers face the challenge of measuring a changing and mobile population. People who are homeless are often on the move, shifting from one form of temporary shelter to another. This makes quantifying homelessness particularly difficult. There have always been some people without homes, but the number of people who are homeless changes over time.

Although not all studies result in the same number, what stands out today is that the number of homeless people in the United States is large and growing. It is also apparent that homelessness affects people of all ages, ethnicities, and social and cultural backgrounds.

THROUGHOUT HISTORY

Historically, the majority of homeless people in America were white men. During the late 1800s through the early 1900s, many were itinerant

workers who traveled from place to place in search of jobs that were often short term. By the mid-1900s, the homeless population shifted to major urban centers. Examples of places where large numbers of homeless people lived at that time include an area of New York City called the Bowery and a district of Los Angeles known as skid row.

During the 1960s, America's homeless population ceased to be primarily white men and began to include African Americans and then Hispanics. During the same time period, the homeless population ceased to be almost exclusively individual males and began to include women and children. By the 1980s, families—most of them headed by single women—became the fastest-growing population of homeless people.

STEREOTYPING

Throughout the history of the United States, those who are poor or without homes have been labeled in negative ways. Labels including *bag lady*, *wino*, *street person*, and *dirty baby* have been used to describe men, women, and children who are homeless. These types of name-calling fuel misunderstanding and negativity. Their use reflects

a common bias against those who are homeless: the misconception that their condition is their own fault. Advocates for the homeless aim to help the public understand that anyone can become homeless and that homelessness is rarely, if ever, a choice that is willingly made.

The idea that homeless people themselves are to blame for their situation has persisted for many centuries. The first almshouses in the United States housed those who were homeless together with criminals, as if they too had committed a crime. Many homeless men in the early twentieth century suffered from alcoholism.

Homeless Veterans

Veterans of the US military make up approximately one-third of the adult homeless population. Many of these veterans suffer from post-traumatic stress syndrome or have physical disabilities resulting from injuries sustained in combat. According to the National Coalition for Homeless Veterans, about half of the veterans who are homeless served during the Vietnam War. But there are homeless veterans of all the major wars fought over the past century including, most recently, the wars in Iraq and Afghanistan.

Herold Noel, a homeless veteran of the Iraq War, was interviewed for the 2008 documentary film *When I Came Home*. In the film he summed up the feelings of homeless veterans: "You never think you are going to leave a war, only to come back home to [fight] a war. The street war."[1]

The National Coalition for Homeless Veterans estimates that an additional 1.5 million veterans are currently living in poverty. Without sufficient support, they too may lose their homes and join the ranks of homeless veterans.

People began using the term *wino* to describe
the homeless, whether a homeless person was an
alcoholic or not. During the Great Depression, a
vast majority of homeless people became homeless
because they lacked sufficient employment. Many
men and some women left their homes and traveled
far and wide in search of work. Their transiency and
poverty gave rise to names such as *tramp* or *bum*.

When homelessness increased steadily in the
1970s and 1980s, women, particularly on the
streets of New York City, carried their possessions
in whatever they could find. Many carried large
bags, which prompted the label of *bag lady*. Despite
the origins of these names, calling a person a bum,
wino, or bag lady is a form of harassment; it hurts
individuals and spreads negativity.

Many Faces

Demographics data of the homeless population
have remained fairly consistent across different
research studies. Individual men remain the largest
population of people who are homeless. In the 2007
US Conference of Mayors report, men represented
approximately 67.5 percent of the total single
homeless population. The single homeless make

up 76 percent of the total homeless
population. Women are also the
heads of many homeless families.
Because of this, women make up
65 percent of homeless people who
are members of households with
children.

Children under the age of 18
make up roughly one-third of the
total homeless population. Most
of them are homeless with their
families. Only a small percentage of
homeless children—approximately
3 to 5 percent—are entirely on their
own. The homeless population
includes a mix of races and
ethnicities. Approximately 60
percent of people who are homeless
are people of color.

Contemporary Homelessness

Contemporary homelessness is
unique from homelessness in the
past in significant ways. In the past,
homelessness has historically tended

**Demographics of the
Sheltered Homeless**

According to the 2009
AHAR, "Sheltered individ-
uals are overwhelmingly
male. More than three
quarters are over 30,
more than 10 percent are
veterans, and more than
40 percent have a dis-
ability. In contrast, adults
in sheltered homeless
families are overwhelm-
ingly female, most are
under age 31, and very
few are veterans or have
a disability. Three-fifths of
the people in homeless
families are children, and
more than half of the children are under age 6."[2]

to grow and shrink with the economy.
In times of prosperity when people
had jobs and economic opportunity,
homelessness abated. When the
economy was bad, such as during the
Great Depression, homelessness was
rampant. The homelessness of today
is more pervasive and long lasting,
according to scholars such as Joel
Blau. In his book *The Visible Poor*, Blau
describes the growth of homelessness
in recent decades:

> *Modern homelessness began in the
> economic difficulties of the 1970s,
> ballooned in the 1981–2 recession, and
> kept on growing despite an economic
> recovery that lasted until the recession of
> the early 1990s.*[3]

Blau cites additional factors
that make the homelessness of
today distinct from that of the past.
These include the decline of social
networks in American communities,
an increase in homelessness in rural

Homeless Population by Ethnicity

The US Conference of Mayors 2006 survey of 25 cities estimated that the homeless population is 42 percent African American, 39 percent white, 13 percent Hispanic, 4 percent Native American, and 2 percent Asian. Compare this with the entire US population—80 percent are white, 13 percent are African American, 4 percent are Asian, 2 percent are two or more races, and 1 percent are Native American. Fifteen percent of the total population is also considered Hispanic.

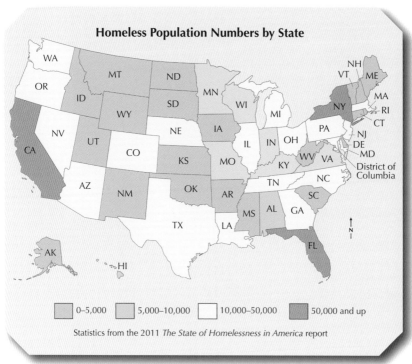

Homeless Population Numbers by State

0–5,000   5,000–10,000   10,000–50,000   50,000 and up

Statistics from the 2011 *The State of Homelessness in America* report

Homeless population numbers vary from state to state.

areas of the country, and a surprising increase in the number of employed people who are homeless in many areas of the country.

During the economic downturn that began in 2007, homelessness has increased again with children and families, who are continuing to be affected in large numbers. Because the most recent data on homelessness does not include this newest

wave, the numbers of homeless people today are likely much larger than previously reported. ⌒

Foreclosure Woes

Since the economic downturn beginning in 2007, there has been a foreclosure crisis in the United States. Foreclosure occurs when homeowners become late in paying their mortgage. After several late or missing payments, the bank takes ownership of the home and residents must move out. According to the 2009 AHAR, "the effect of the foreclosure crisis on homelessness seems to be mainly indirect, reflected by the increase in the percentage of families that had been staying with relatives before they became homeless. The change between 2008 and 2009 in the number who said they had been staying with family before becoming homeless was about 9,500, and the three-year change between 2007 and 2009 was 27,330."[4]

*Veterans make up a large percentage
of the homeless population in the United States.*

Lack of affordable housing, such as the Riverton Houses complex in Harlem, New York, is one cause of homelessness.

CAUSES OF HOMELESSNESS

There is no single reason why one person becomes homeless and another person does not. It is not a person's choice to be homeless. Homelessness is a condition that can result from a series of events or from one major catastrophe.

Once homeless, people face a debilitating cycle that is very difficult to break.

A variety of factors can contribute to homelessness. The primary causes are poverty and lack of affordable housing. Various other conditions, both physical and mental, are also triggers for homelessness. They include the loss of a job, a natural disaster, mental illness, lack of community or family support, addiction, domestic violence, and chronic unemployment. The majority of homeless people suffer from a combination of these conditions. For example, a poor woman who is a victim of domestic violence might not have any resources or family to depend on when she leaves an abusive husband. An alcoholic might have had a good job but has been fired and may have exhausted the support of friends and family before winding up on the streets.

KELLY'S STORY

Most people think of homeless men and women as having suffered severe social and personal tragedies such as domestic violence, drug addiction, or mental illness. While that is often true, the story is not always so dramatic. Many newly homeless

in the United States today had jobs, homes, and a network of support until a sudden change in luck landed them on the street.

Kelly Robinson, a writer who was formerly homeless, recorded her experience to foster awareness about the plight of homelessness and to put a face on what is often an anonymous tragedy. Robinson was artistic and had a good education. She had been fortunate to have a variety of job opportunities, but her adventurous spirit led her to change jobs often. When Robinson was in her early forties, she moved to a new city by herself to start a new job.

Mr. Allesandro's Story

In his book *Rachel and Her Children*, author Jonathan Kozol tells the story of an Italian-American family he met in a New York City homeless shelter. The father of the family, Mr. Allesandro, held a job as a maintenance man. When his wife left him and their three children, he could no longer make it to work on time because he had to get the children ready for school. To keep his job, Allesandro took a part-time shift. But the pay was not enough to meet his rent. Soon the family was evicted.

Allesandro's family was placed in a large shelter with no private bedrooms or dividing curtains. To arrive at work on time, Allesandro would have had to leave his children alone in the shelter every morning before school, which he feared was unsafe. Allesandro was unable to make it to work and he lost his job.

Eventually, Allesandro's family was placed in a welfare hotel. Allesandro said, "I can do construction, carpentry. I can repair things. I'm somebody who's mechanically inclined. I would make beds. I would clean toilets. I'd do anything if I could have a decent job."[1]

She was staying in a motel, preparing to go in for her first day of work, when she got a call informing her that her job had been eliminated. Robinson was devastated—she had no savings and did not know anyone in the town. Her minivan became her home. Robinson described her shock at finding herself homeless:

> *I went from employed with a place to live to unemployed with no home in the blink of an eye, and that resourceful side of me that always saw a way out was temporarily blinded. . . . I would never again feel fully safe. I would never again be fooled into believing that homelessness happens to other people. I still feel, to this day, that I have one foot in the door and one foot just inches away from no longer having a door.* [2]

INDIVIDUAL AND STRUCTURAL PERSPECTIVES

There are different sets of beliefs about what causes a person to be homeless. Perspectives on homelessness that have emerged since the 1980s fall into two main categories: the individual and the structural.

The individual perspective asserts that homelessness is the result of personal failings

or disabilities. A book from the
National Coalition for the Homeless
describes this perspective:

> *According to this perspective, people were homeless because something was wrong with them. They were severely mentally ill, for instance, or end-of-the-line substance abusers—people unable to care for themselves, unable to keep themselves housed, and newly visible because of drastic changes in policies that had previously kept them institutionalized in hospitals or jails.*[3]

The structural perspective asserts that homelessness is a result of social and economic problems such as high unemployment levels and high housing costs:

> *The other explanation put forward was that pervasive and rising homelessness was caused by structural factors; that is, that it was a function of the way our society's resources are organized and distributed.*[4]

A Safety Net

As rents have increased while salaries and public support have not, more and more Americans are forced to live from paycheck to paycheck. These families pay their basic expenses and do not have anything left for savings. In many cases, they cannot afford insurance against a natural disaster or a medical emergency. Without savings or insurance as a safety net, a family is at risk of becoming homeless within a month or two of losing their main source of income.

2010 Minimum Wage Jobs Needed Per Household

WA: 2.1*
OR: 1.8*
MT: 1.7
ND: 1.6
MN: 2.1
NH: 2.7 ME: 2.1*
VT: 2.2*
ID: 1.8
WY: 1.9
SD: 1.6
WI: 2.0
MA: 2.9*
NY: 3.3
RI: 2.6*
CT: 2.8*
NV: 2.6*
UT: 2.0
NE: 1.8
IA: 1.7
MI: 1.9
PA: 2.2
NJ: 3.4
CA: 3.2*
CO: 2.3
IL: 1.9
IN: 1.9
OH: 1.8*
DE: 2.7
MD: 3.4
KS: 1.8
WV: 1.6
VA: 2.7
DC: 3.5*
AZ: 2.3
NM: 1.8
OK: 1.7
MO: 1.8
KY: 1.7
NC: 1.9
AR: 1.6
TN: 1.9
SC: 1.9
MS: 1.8
AL: 1.7
GA: 2.1
TX: 2.2
LA: 2.1
FL: 2.8*
AK: 2.8
HI: 4.3

N

Jobs at Minimum Wage

More than 3 jobs   2–3 jobs   Fewer than 2 jobs

Note: States are classified by the unrounded number of minimum wage jobs required to rent a two-bedroom apartment at 30 percent of income.
* State's minimum wage exceeds federal minimum wage of $7.25.

Source: National Low Income Housing Coalition

In some states, more than three people in a family need to work full-time jobs at minimum wage to afford the rent of a two-bedroom apartment.

Those who take the structural perspective cite the growing gap between the rich and the poor and the dramatic decrease in affordable housing. According to the US Department of Housing and Urban Development, affordable housing should cost no more than 30 percent of a household's annual income. So, if a family's annual income is $40,000, they should pay no more than $12,000 each year in rent or mortgage payments. However, it is estimated that 12 million Americans pay more than 50 percent

of their annual income for housing. If there is only one full-time worker in a family and that person earns the minimum wage, which ranges from $5.15 to $8.67 per hour in states that require a minimum wage, the family cannot afford to rent a two-bedroom apartment anywhere in the United States.

Some cite the faulty logic of the individual approach. Certainly some homeless people have mental illnesses or disabilities that make it hard for them to maintain a home on their own, and others abuse alcohol or have made unfortunate employment choices. But plenty of people with homes have had these issues for decades. Although these factors are relevant to the homeless population, they do not necessarily lead directly to homelessness.

There are also concerns with the structural approach. Explaining the causes of homelessness accurately is essential so that policy responses will address the right problems. Critics of the structural perspective argue that if individual problems such as mental illness, substance abuse, or lack of job training are not addressed, then people with these problems will remain homeless.

A balanced approach integrates individual and structural factors. A perspective on the causes of

homelessness that takes into account both individual concerns and the structure of the socioeconomic system as a whole allows support providers and homeless advocates to assess what kinds of help individuals need and to secure funding for meaningful assistance. Although both purely structural and purely individual explanations have been made in the past, the most widely supported explanation among researchers is an integrated approach.

LACK OF AFFORDABLE HOUSING

Historically, evidence supports the claim that lack of housing is the primary cause of homelessness. Affordable housing has been on the decline in the United States since at least the 1980s. Scholars studying the phenomenon of homelessness cite the economics of the 1980s as the source of the rising tide of homelessness that continues today.

"The lack of affordable housing is a significant hardship for low-income households preventing them from meeting their other basic needs, such as nutrition and healthcare, or saving for their future and that of their families."[5]
—US Department of Housing and Urban Development

Changes in the federal tax structure and other federal policies combined to create a significant drop in affordable housing in the 1980s. The Economic Recovery Tax Act of 1981 cut 25 percent of income taxes over three years. This left less public money for social programs, including government housing. Corporations were given assistance in the form of tax breaks and other economic incentives to build more new housing at the expense of low-cost housing. The federal government also cut personnel at the Consumer Product Safety Commission and the Occupational Safety and Health Administration (OSHA). With fewer employees, these regulatory bodies were not as effective. Corporations, including construction and development companies, became less regulated. In many cities, low-cost housing was torn down and replaced with new developments, displacing large numbers of people.

At the same time, federal funds for public housing were scaled back and more people were renting homes. These and other factors combined to inflate costs for renters and dramatically decrease the availability of public or affordable housing.

INCOME DISPARITY

While rental prices were increasing, both incomes and federal funds for the poor were dropping. Between 1970 and 1988, the number of people classified as poor grew from 25.4 million to 31.9 million. Meanwhile, new regulations favorable to business increased incomes at the highest levels, but not at the lower levels. Even for those with jobs, wages did not keep up with the rising cost of living. This meant that even as rent and food prices continued to increase, incomes did not.

In *The Visible Poor*, Joel Blau describes the resulting income gap between the wealthy and the poor:

> *In one typical study, the Congressional Budget Office (CBO) estimated that between 1980 and 1990, the income of the poorest tenth of U.S. households decreased by 8.6%, to an average of $4,695. At the other end of the income*

On the Margins

Living in poverty puts a person at an increased risk of becoming homeless. According to the National Coalition for Homelessness, 12.5 percent of the US population, or 37 million people, lived in poverty in 2007. Of those living in poverty, 35.7 percent were children.

range, families did much better. The top fifth increased its income by 29.8%, the top 5 percent by 44.9%; and the richest 1 percent by 75.3%, to an average of $548,969.[6]

The growing divide between rich and poor and the incidence of homelessness are interconnected. One of the more direct ways to understand it is through the redevelopment of urban areas. Throughout the nation, corporations, newly wealthy from tax breaks and less prone to federal safety citations due to pared down regulatory bodies, went to work building new developments including homes and condominiums. Where land was scarce, as it was in most big cities, older low-cost housing was torn down to make way for the new construction. In the process, people, families in particular, were displaced in large numbers. Many of these displaced people continued to work at low wage or menial jobs but could not afford the high cost of rent on a new home or the high cost to relocate to a different city that may have had more employment opportunities.

Minimum- to low-wage jobs, such as working at a car wash, do not provide enough income to meet housing costs.

For some homeless people, alcohol abuse is a problem.

Homelessness
and Health

A common myth about homelessness is that all homeless people are addicted to drugs or alcohol or are mentally ill. This is untrue, but there are certainly homeless people that have one or both of these conditions. For those providing

services to the homeless (such as shelter workers, doctors, volunteers, social workers, and others), it is important to know whether a homeless individual is suffering from addiction or mental illness in order to provide the right kind of support.

Just as it is difficult to get an accurate number of the homeless, determining just how many are mentally ill or have addictions is challenging. Assessing a series of studies, Joel Blau surmised that "[a]bout one-quarter to one-third of the homeless population suffers from severe mental illness."[1] Other sources state that statistic to be slightly lower, at 20 to 25 percent. Either way, the percentage is dramatic considering that out of the entire US population, only approximately 6 percent have been diagnosed as mentally ill.

A slightly higher percentage of homeless people are addicted to alcohol or drugs. According to data collected from 30 cities in the US Conference of Mayors' study of homelessness, the number of homeless people addicted to drugs or alcohol varied significantly from city to city. It found that more than 50 percent of the homeless population in Boston, Cleveland, and New Orleans were addicted to drugs or alcohol, while less than 20 percent in

Chicago, Nashville, and San Antonio suffered from addictions. On average, approximately one-third of the homeless population suffered from addiction to alcohol or drugs.

The Road to Recovery

Recognizing the acute health-care needs of the homeless, the Baltimore-based nonprofit organization Healthcare for the Homeless (HCH) provides medical services to homeless people. Approximately 50 percent of their clients suffer from addiction, 34 percent have a mental illness, and approximately 25 percent have a dual diagnosis.

People who come to HCH receive two kinds of help. First, they get health care in the form of medical and counseling services, and secondly, they receive practical aid in finding housing. The stories of former clients demonstrate the power of this combined approach. Before finding HCH, Celeste and Robert were unemployed, homeless, and addicted to drugs. They suffered from addiction for 25 years. Because of their longtime drug use, the couple's three children were taken from them for a time by the state child protective services agency.

Celeste and Robert received health care and counseling services at HCH. They were eventually able to find jobs and rent a home, and their children were returned to them. As Celeste said of their journey out of addiction and homelessness, "It's like starting your life all over again. And basically that is what I have done; that's what both of us have done."[2]

THE MENTALLY ILL

Changes in mental health care occurred during the mid-1960s and 1970s. Prior to that time, most people with mental illnesses were kept in mental hospitals. A strong patients' rights movement, which advocated for less restrictive health care for the mentally ill, led to numerous patients being released into the general public, where they could be

*Joseph Rogers, left, worked with a mental health group
that assisted homeless and deinstitutionalized people on the streets.*

integrated into communities. This process, known
as deinstitutionalization, occurred in cities across
the country. For example, in New York, 126,000
patients were released from state hospitals between
the years 1965 and 1979. While implementing this
new policy, many states failed to create the housing
and community programs that were needed to
support the mentally ill.

For many years, deinstitutionalization was
considered to be a cause of homelessness, but more
recent data has shown otherwise. First, the majority

of patients who were released from mental hospitals did not end up homeless. Second, the fastest growing population of homeless people were families, not individuals who were mentally ill.

MENTAL ILLNESS AND HOMELESSNESS

While being mentally ill does not guarantee that a person will become homeless, it can make a person more vulnerable to homelessness, particularly when combined with poverty or the lack of a supportive network of family and friends.

People with a mental illness often struggle to maintain order in their lives. An incident that might be a minor setback to a mentally healthy person, such as a lost check or a missing set of keys, has the potential to disrupt the fragile order of daily life for someone with a mental illness. This vulnerability is exacerbated by homelessness. Having a mental illness can make it even harder for a person to find shelter, food, friends, and to accept support.

The Soloist

The 2009 movie, *The Soloist*, is based on a book by *Los Angeles Times* newspaper columnist Steve Lopez. It tells the true story of the reporter's friendship with a talented musician named Nathaniel Ayers who is both mentally ill and homeless. Ayers was once a student at Juilliard, the famous music school in New York City. At 21, he was diagnosed with schizophrenia, a long term and severe mental disorder. *The Soloist* shines a light on how the mentally ill can easily fall through the cracks of health-care systems and housing systems to end up homeless.

In addition, some researchers argue that homelessness is so stressful that it can by itself cause mental illness or symptoms similar to those of mental illness. Homelessness is an extremely taxing condition that can create deep anxiety and depression. It can also lead to what would, for a housed person, be considered strange or odd behavior. As Joel Blau noted:

> The principle reference book of the American Psychiatric Association says that collecting garbage, hoarding food, and a marked impairment in personal hygiene and grooming are residual symptoms of schizophrenia. Perhaps they are, but perhaps they are also not-so-residual symptoms of lacking a home.[3]

The connection between mental illness and homelessness is complicated. One does not cause the other, but both are deeply challenging conditions for the human psyche. For those who suffer from them simultaneously, the challenges are immense.

ADDICTION

Alcoholism has long been associated with homelessness. For many years, alcoholism was not understood. As a result, people suffering from this illness had few options for treatment. In the

early part of the twentieth century, alcoholism was prevalent mostly among white men who made up the homeless population.

Street drugs are a more recent problem affecting the homeless. Until the mid-1980s, illegal drugs were very expensive and therefore much less likely to be found among the homeless population than alcohol. But during the 1980s, an inexpensive drug called crack cocaine became available and was sold in poor neighborhoods of metropolitan areas. In his book *The Homeless*, author Christopher Jencks makes a connection between the introduction of crack cocaine and the rise of homelessness during the 1980s. Citing a study that showed as many as half of the homeless people in New York were using crack, Jencks surmised, "that may help explain the otherwise puzzling increase in homelessness between 1984 and 1988, when unemployment was falling."[4]

Addiction to drugs or alcohol makes it very difficult to maintain a job or relationships. For this reason, people with these addictions are also vulnerable to homelessness. And as with mental illness, the risk is greatest when the person affected is also poor. If a drug addict has limited income, he or she must choose between spending money on rent

or drugs. Addiction can also exacerbate homelessness once a person is on the streets. Whether the income comes from a job, federal support, or charity, spending all of it on drugs or alcohol leaves nothing left for food, shelter, and other basic necessities.

DUAL DIAGNOSES AND INTEGRATED TREATMENT

Mental illness and substance abuse are distinct from one another. However, the National Alliance of Mental Illness (NAMI) has found that they often occur simultaneously. According to NAMI,

> *Roughly 50 percent of individuals with severe mental disorders are affected by substance abuse. Thirty-seven percent of alcohol abusers and 53 percent of drug abusers also have at least one serious mental illness.*[5]

When both mental illness and substance abuse are present, this is referred to as a dual diagnosis. Studies have shown that dual diagnoses are best treated with an integrated

Homelessness and HIV/AIDS

According to the National Coalition for the Homeless, HIV infection and AIDS are connected with homelessness. HIV medications are very expensive and require consistent use to be effective. People with HIV also suffer from job loss due to discrimination. The combination of job loss and expensive medication puts many people with HIV/AIDS at risk of losing their homes. The stress and insecurity of poverty and homelessness can also accelerate the symptoms of HIV/AIDS, making people get sicker faster.

approach that treats both conditions at the same time.

Case Management

Social workers and other service providers use a process called case management to address the multiple needs of a homeless person who is mentally ill, addicted, or who has a dual diagnosis. In case management, one individual or a team of service providers stays with the person who is being served throughout the course of his or her treatment.

In addition, studies have shown that a similar form of integrated treatment is most successful in supporting homeless people with mental illness, substance abuse, or dual diagnoses. In short, though they are different conditions, very similar forms of treatment have been shown to be successful with both populations.

Treatment is not a one-size-fits-all approach; service providers get to know each individual and understand his or her needs and concerns. Other features of successful treatment include long-term support and follow-up services.

Other people with mental illness or addiction who have successfully overcome homelessness are particularly helpful in aiding those who are homeless. They provide a hopeful example and real understanding for those who are facing a difficult path.

*Drug treatment helped Candice Singer move
from homelessness to her own home.*

*In 2008, homeless New Yorkers rallied
at the Federal Plaza for more Section 8 housing in the city.*

SEEKING SHELTER

acking the basic necessities of everyday life,
people who are homeless are forced to find
refuge and sustenance in other ways. Providing the
homeless with a place to live, eat, and bathe is the first
priority in alleviating the effects of homelessness.

Private, nonprofit, and governmental agencies for the homeless have addressed the need of housing in different ways. Government initiatives, such as a federal program called Section 8, provide assistance to those unable to afford rental or mortgage payments. But these programs are not always successful. Funds for Section 8 vouchers are limited and there are far more people in need of them than there are available vouchers. There are many requirements for acceptance into the program, and even once a person is accepted, it can be a challenge to find housing since not all landlords agree to accept Section 8 vouchers.

Other programs provide temporary shelter to those who are homeless. Some local governments commit to providing shelter for all who need it, while others have no such commitment. But several studies have determined that the amount of shelter beds in any given city is significantly lower than the amount of people who are homeless. Studies have also shown that many shelters have inadequate space for their areas' needs or are

"Of the 25 cities surveyed by the US Conference of Mayors for its annual Hunger and Homelessness Report, 19 reported an increase in homelessness in 2008. On average, cities reported a 12 percent increase. The lack of available shelter space leaves many homeless persons with no choice but to struggle to survive on the streets of our cities."[1]
   —*City Mayors Society, July 2009*

unsafe due to violence between residents. As a result, people who are homeless sometimes opt to live on the street rather than stay in a shelter.

UNSHELTERED HOMELESS

Some homeless people create their own shelter. They sleep in cardboard boxes, tents, or in other kinds of makeshift structures placed outside or in abandoned buildings. Life on the street means facing serious safety concerns. Aside from being vulnerable to violent crime, people living on the streets suffer from insect and rodent bites, exposure to extreme heat and cold, and near-constant hunger. Accidents, theft, and lack of health care add to the challenges of life on the street.

Although living on the streets has never been considered safe, evidence has shown that violence against the homeless has been on the rise in recent years in the form of hate crimes. A hate crime is a violent attack on someone based on personal or ethnic

Tent Cities

Tent cities have been established by the homeless in areas around the United States. A "tent city" is an area where people build or set up temporary housing facilities, such as tents or wooden shacks. Once called shantytowns or Hoovervilles, these areas have been in existence since the Great Depression. Tent cities can be either sanctioned by the government or illegal in different parts of the country. Larger encampments are sometimes named, such as Dignity Village in Portland, Oregon. Some have community gardens and specific rules for residents to follow.

A homeless man called "Grandpa" is a resident of the tent city in Portland, Oregon, called Dignity Village.

characteristics. In September 2010, the US Senate Judiciary Committee held a special hearing to examine the incidence of hate crimes against homeless people. Its goal was to assist the Federal Bureau of Investigation in collecting data on the issue.

EMERGENCY AND DAY SHELTERS

Emergency shelters provide a place to sleep for one night. These generally consist of one or more large rooms with beds and a common bathroom. There is little to no privacy or storage space and the shelters are generally open only at night.

Day shelters are spaces that provide a place for homeless people to go during the day. These facilities generally have bathrooms and showers and offer services including job training and drug counseling. Some day shelters offer quiet spaces, such as a reading or music room, to sit and relax. And some offer spaces for community meetings, gatherings, and cultural events, such as a writers' group.

Funding for emergency and day shelters varies. Nonprofit groups, churches, and private organizations provide funding and space for shelters. One of the biggest providers of emergency shelter nationwide is the Salvation Army. Cities nationwide also run and operate shelters for the homeless. Shelters are funded by a combination of federal, state, and municipal funds; private donations; and grants.

Transitional Housing

Transitional housing is a type of shelter focused on moving households to permanent housing.

They are open day and night. Though it is not the same as having a home of one's own, transitional housing offers a more lasting solution for a homeless person. But there are limits to how long one can stay in transitional housing. The average stay is six months to two years. Transitional housing is intended to be a stepping-stone from homelessness to permanent housing.

Unlike the majority of homeless shelters, which are free, residents typically pay a fee for transitional housing. Most in transitional shelters receive government assistance, which goes toward paying

Short on Space

Across the country, there is not enough space in shelters for the number of homeless people seeking refuge. With the recent recession, homelessness has increased again, making for even more crowding in shelters. In December 2009, the *Chicago Tribune* reported that homeless shelters in and around Chicago were forced to turn away hundreds of people for lack of room. Even traditionally wealthy suburban areas showed an increase in the homeless population.

The *Tribune* reported, "surveys don't capture the grim truth on the streets and at shelters—emergency beds are scarce. From Chicago Heights to Waukegan, demand has outstripped supply, with shelters resorting to lotteries and free bus passes out of town to handle the overflow."[3]

In August 2010, the *Los Angeles Times* cited "overwhelming demand [for shelter space] triggered by the recession and recurring visits by some guests" in explaining that one of the city's largest emergency shelters, The Union Rescue Mission, would begin charging a fee from guests who could afford to pay.[4]

"About 44 million Americans—one in seven —lived last year in homes in which the income was below the poverty level, which is about $22,000 for a family of four. That is the largest number of people since the census began tracking poverty 51 years ago."[5]
—Washington Post, September 2010

the fee. As with shelters, there is not enough transitional housing available for the number of people in need.

Transitional housing is available for both individuals and families. Some transitional housing offers shelter only to particular populations, such as women with children or women fleeing domestic violence. Specifying the clientele they serve limits availability but allows organizations to tailor services to a particular population.

Housing, whether it is a temporary shelter or transitional housing, is a critical step toward regaining independence and stability. Simply having a permanent address can open many doors. Employment becomes more of a possibility, and school enrollment for children is easier. But the lack of available shelter space and affordable housing forces many to live on the streets. While creating more shelters and affordable housing would reduce the number of homeless on the streets, some believe making living in public spaces a crime is an appropriate response.

The Charles Cobb apartment complex, part of the Skid Row Housing Trust in Los Angeles, California, provides transitional housing.

Homeless activists protest against the criminalization of the homeless in Los Angeles, California.

SOLUTIONS
AND PREVENTION

People who are homeless have the same needs as anyone else; they need shelter, food, and friends. But because they cannot find or maintain affordable housing, they must fulfill these basic needs in a public way. The public nature of

their struggle triggers a wide variety of responses and emotions in society. These responses range from compassion to aggression. At one end of the spectrum, neighborhood and community groups donate provisions, serve food, or provide shelter to those who are homeless. At the other end of the spectrum, hate crimes against homeless people are on the rise.

Seeing a homeless person can trigger a complex set of emotions that can include sadness, fear, and guilt. But advocates point out that the more society understands homelessness, the less likely people are to stereotype and stigmatize the homeless. Advocacy groups such as the National Coalition for the Homeless work to educate society about homelessness. One of the points these groups emphasize is that there is no single reason why people become homeless and no single solution to the complex problem.

The Law

The public nature of homelessness has led law enforcement to become involved in a variety of ways. Historically, US police stations have set up temporary shelters for the homeless. As homelessness

has increased over time, local police forces also find themselves enforcing laws that limit the ways homeless people can live in public spaces.

Attorney Harry Simon summarized the conflict between law and advocacy in an essay for the National Coalition for the Homeless:

> *In city after city, municipal decisions to use criminal [punishments] to protect public spaces have come into conflict with efforts by civil rights advocates to prevent the criminalization of homelessness.*[1]

For example, the city of San Diego, California, banned any form of lodging in public or private spaces without permission. For those unable to find space in a homeless shelter, this law effectively made homelessness illegal.

When laws arc passed against sleeping or spending time in public spaces, homeless people are arrested and jailed. A punitive approach

Homelessness Each Year in US Cities

• In Chicago, one person in 1,810 is homeless.
• In New York, one person in 2,688 is homeless.
• In Los Angeles, one person in 154 is homeless.
• In Washington DC, one person in 1,844 is homeless.

to homelessness adds another level to the cycle of poverty and misfortune. An example can be seen in the story of a 12-year-old homeless girl named Angelina. The girl stole food out of desperate hunger, but was arrested like a criminal. "When they caught her stealin' at the store," her mother told author Jonathan Kozol, "they brought her here in handcuffs. I don't think you need to do that to a child. Once you see that . . . you see your own self different from before."[2]

The law presents an additional challenge for homeless adolescents. Children and teens are legally required to have a guardian, so adolescents who have run away from abusive families or foster homes can be arrested as status offenders. Although they have not broken any laws, their status of being homeless and underage is a crime. Rather than being sent to a shelter, these teens are placed in detention facilities with other adolescents who have broken the law. While they may not have to return home, homeless adolescents are placed in a different dangerous environment where they may experience violence or be negatively influenced by real criminals.

COMMUNITY SOLUTIONS

While some cities have passed laws that adversely affect the homeless, many have also been more effective at delivering services than state or federal governments. According to homeless expert Joel Blau,

> *The social movement for the homeless has lobbied for assistance at every level of government, but in practice, it is cities that deliver most of the benefits and services. The federal and state governments normally fund part of this aid. Yet by the time the homeless actually get assistance, the money has generally been handed down to the local government, which may, or may not, add its own tax revenues.*[3]

Local aid to the homeless mostly comes from local governments, but also private and nonprofit groups. They provide services ranging from shelter and food to job training and drug counseling. Many of these services are sponsored and administered by the city. For example, in the city of Los Angeles, the Los Angeles Homeless Services Authority (LAHSA) is jointly run by the city and county of Los Angeles. LAHSA receives and administers federal and state funds to provide services to the homeless community. It provides integrated treatment to help the homeless access housing and receive assistance,

while also providing information and education about the homeless population.

Like other American cities, Los Angeles is host to numerous local groups that aid the homeless and are run by churches, private groups, nonprofits, or community centers. Often, these types of groups work together. For example, a church group that wants to help the homeless would most likely collaborate with a local nonprofit organization to provide meals or donate clothing. Schools often host fundraisers or drives to collect toys, socks, toiletries, or other necessities for the homeless. These are then given to a local service provider that can distribute the collected items to those in need.

PREVENTION AND HOUSING

Prevention is a key strategy in the fight to end homelessness. Rent assistance, housing services, and budget counseling are part of preventative services. Rent assistance comes in the form of a payment of the first month's rent and deposit or paying back rent owed to a landlord.

"With the growing number of homeless families and individuals in America, states have developed policies and programs to address the problem. Working through local governments and nonprofit organizations, states distribute funds—often, funds granted to them by the federal government—to an array of programs and services to help homeless people."[4]
—*Author Vicky Watson in Homelessness in America*

To encourage these types of assistance, the US Congress and President Barack Obama approved the Homelessness Prevention and Rapid Re-Housing Program on February 17, 2009. This $1.5 billion program is part of the American Recovery and Reinvestment Act, which gives funds to communities across the nation in support of homelessness prevention services and rapid re-housing assistance. It can be the critical help needed to stop individuals and families from becoming homeless.

An example of a successful prevention program can be seen in Hennepin County in Minnesota. Its Rapid Exit Program, which is primarily federally funded, finances homelessness prevention services. These services include legal services needed for eviction court cases, case management, volunteer assistance to help families keep housing, financial help, and mediation services between tenant and landlord. Using these services helps tenants stay in their homes and reduces or eliminates their need to stay in emergency shelters.

Public housing is another option for people at risk of homelessness. It is owned by the government and is available at a reduced rate. The average stay in public housing is three to five years. According

Funds are raised to support organizations that serve homeless populations in a 2010 walkathon in Washington DC.

to the US Department of Housing and Urban Development (HUD),

> Public housing comes in all sizes and types, from scattered single family houses to highrise apartments for elderly families. There are approximately 1.2 million households living in public housing units, managed by some 3,300 [housing agencies].[5]

Through HUD, the federal government provides funding for public housing and the local planning and development of public housing.

Public housing has been a controversial solution. It provides a more long-lasting alternative than emergency shelters, but it too can be unsafe. For example, the Nickerson Gardens housing project in Los Angeles, the largest public housing facility in the United States, struggles with persistent gang activity in and around the facility. Children living in Nickerson Gardens are regular witnesses to violence and drug use.

The need for housing is so great that, despite safety concerns, waiting lists for public housing are long. It can take up to 20 years to get into a public housing unit.

What Can Individuals Do?

Individuals can respond to the issue of homelessness in a variety of ways. Some feel guilty, others ignore the issue, and still others find ways to help. Individuals tend to ignore the homeless out of guilt, fear, or misunderstanding. But as people learn more about homelessness, they are more likely to accept and acknowledge people who are homeless. Even a simple human interaction, such as a wave, can provide a sense of belonging to a person who is homeless and feels disconnected from society.

The first thing service providers offer someone who is homeless is food, such as a sandwich or juice. This helps to meet a basic need for the person who is homeless, but it also provides an icebreaker for conversation that can lead to assistance.

Community volunteers use a similar method, spending time at soup kitchens to offer food to the homeless and, over time, getting to know the homeless. Basic conversations and interactions between service providers, volunteers, and clients begin to establish a sense of belonging that can be beneficial for someone who is homeless.

Homelessness continues to increase in cities, towns, and rural areas of the United States. This complex and growing social

A Volunteer's Story

Joan Curtain is a volunteer at a homeless shelter in Hollywood, California. Each week since 2004, she has collaborated with other volunteers to serve meals to people who are homeless. "I have been moved every time in my life that I have encountered someone sleeping on a bus stop bench, or under a carport for shelter from the rain, or asking for spare change," she explained. "It is always to me a wake-up call: I am so blessed and take so much for granted. So I thought maybe it was time I did something with those feelings."[6]

At first, Curtain worked with only two other members of her church. Each week they fed approximately 40 people who were homeless. Today, the group has grown to 60 volunteers, some from Curtain's church and others from the neighborhood. They feed up to 140–200 people every Saturday and up to 400 people on Thanksgiving and Christmas.

An Ethnographic Lens

An ethnographic study is a form of study in which the researcher lives in and among the people he or she is researching. In ethnographic studies of people who are homeless, researchers live on the streets and in shelters. They can then study the experiences of the homeless through their own personal experiences, providing an in-depth view of the issue. The ethnographic method provides a better opportunity for researchers to closely document homelessness and allows for longer observation and interviewing times.

issue affects many. The homeless can be seen on the streets in cities and towns around the country. They are brothers, sisters, uncles, or parents. They struggle to meet their most basic needs and fight to survive on the streets. There is no simple solution to the problem of homelessness. Preventative services and federal involvement are essential in order to make progress in the struggle. In 2010, the federal government committed to preventing and ending chronic homelessness in the United States. These goals include, among others, an increase in affordable housing, greater leadership and involvement from the government, and more employment opportunities for those at risk of homelessness. With a combination of these commitments and public understanding, fewer individuals and families may experience homelessness in the future.

Habitat for Humanity is a volunteer-driven organization
that helps alleviate homelessness by building affordable housing.

TIMELINE

Mid-1800s	1839	1850
Care for the homeless shifts from domestic and community based care to local or state governments and police stations.	New York sets up an asylum for mentally ill and disabled homeless people	New York City constructs an almshouse.

1935	1963	1965–1979
The Social Security Act is passed.	President Lyndon Johnson expands funding for public assistance programs.	Deinstitutionalization allows for the release of patients from state mental hospitals across the country.

1930s

The Great Depression causes widespread poverty, job loss, and homelessness.

1932

President Franklin D. Roosevelt is elected when 13 million people are unemployed in the United States.

1932

President Roosevelt introduces legislation designed to aid the poor, jobless, homeless, and elderly.

1979

In the *Callahan v. Carey* legal battle, a New York court orders the state to provide shelter for all homeless men.

1980s

Crack cocaine addiction becomes a widespread problem among the poor and homeless populations.

1982

The National Coalition for the Homeless is founded in New York City.

TIMELINE

1983	1986	1987
The National Governors Association task force on homelessness recommends increased federal support.	The Homeless Persons' Survival Act is drafted by several organizations.	The Stewart B. McKinney Homeless Assistance Act is passed in July.

1994	2007	2009
Congress amends the McKinney Act to ensure that children who are homeless attend school.	A US economic recession begins, leading to foreclosures and increases in homelessness.	On February 17, the Homelessness Prevention and Rapid Re-Housing Program is enacted.

1988

The McKinney Act is amended with minor changes.

1990

Congress amends the McKinney Act, expanding services to the homeless.

1992

The McKinney Act is amended for a third time and new programs are created to serve the homeless.

2009

The Homeless Emergency and Rapid Transition to Housing (HEARTH) Act becomes law in May.

2010

The US government releases its goals for ending chronic homelessness.

ESSENTIAL FACTS

AT ISSUE

❖ To be homeless means to be without a home. The emotional, psychological, and physical implications of homelessness are severe. People who are homeless must look to the public sphere to meet their most basic needs for food, shelter, and sanitation.

❖ People of every age, race, and background are homeless. The US Conference of Mayors 2006 survey of 25 cities estimated that the homeless population is 42 percent African American, 39 percent white, 13 percent Hispanic, 4 percent Native American, and 2 percent Asian.

❖ The primary cause of homelessness is lack of affordable housing for those living in poverty. Additional factors that exacerbate homelessness include a loss of income; lack of support from family, friends or coworkers; mental illness; and substance abuse.

❖ City, state, and federal government programs provide services to support those who are homeless. These services include access to temporary shelter, aid to transition into more permanent housing, counseling, social services, food, and other basic needs. Despite this aid, there are not enough shelter beds for everyone who is homeless, and those that receive federal funds often do not receive a sufficient amount to afford basic housing.

CRITICAL DATES

1987
In July, the first major federal legislation to aid those who are homeless, the Stewart B. McKinney Act, is passed.

1990
Congress amends the McKinney Act to significantly expand services to the homeless. The Community Mental Health Services program becomes Projects for Assistance in Transition from Homelessness (PATH) to reflect the new focus on homeless issues.

1994

Congress amends and expands the McKinney Act to ensure that children who are homeless attend school.

2009

In May, President Barack Obama signs the Homeless Emergency and Rapid Transition to Housing (HEARTH) Act into law, expanding support for the rural homeless and increasing support for resources to prevent homelessness nationwide.

QUOTES

"The social movement to house the homeless sees homelessness as a social problem rather than a private trouble. Politics replaces charity. Food, clothing, and shelter are no longer donations to the unfortunate. Instead, in this movement, advocates see the necessities of life as a basic human right." —*Joel Blau, author of* The Visible Poor

"I went from employed with a place to live to unemployed with no home in the blink of an eye, and that resourceful side of me that always saw a way out was temporarily blinded."—*Writer and former homeless person Kelly Robinson*

"It should never be forgotten, and that's how I survive every day with as little judgment as humanly possible. I never forget that it could be me tomorrow that is living on the street, that is homeless, that has mental health issues."— *Staff member at Women Street Survivors Resource Group, a shelter for homeless women*

GLOSSARY

addiction
> A compulsive need to use a drug or other substance that is psychologically or physically habit-forming and harmful to the user.

advocate
> One that stands up for or defends another.

alcoholism
> The addiction to alcohol; a psychological and physical addiction that brings on withdrawal symptoms if the user stops taking in alcohol and that has many health risks.

almshouse
> A historic name for a homeless shelter.

anthropologist
> A scientist who studies human beings, typically focused on one particular time or era, such as the study of people who are homeless at a given time in history.

foreclosure
> The legal termination of an individual's ownership of land or property, usually due to a failure to make loan payments.

Great Depression
> A period of intense and widespread economic time in the United States during the 1930s.

nonprofit
> A group designed for social or cultural goals and not for profit.

poverty
> The lack of sufficient funds to pay for housing, food, and other basic needs.

public assistance
> Government aid to people in need, such as the elderly or the poor.

public housing

Government-funded long-term housing for the poor and homeless.

recession

A time period with reduced or diminished economic activity, usually characterized by widespread job loss and spending cuts.

shelter

Any place that provides temporary shelter to people who are homeless.

skid row

The name given to an area with a high concentration of shelters, temporary homes, and makeshift dwellings where homeless people tend to congregate.

social worker

A professional dedicated to providing a variety of services, from direct to organizational, to populations that are in need or disadvantaged.

soup kitchen

A place that donates and serves basic meals to the hungry and homeless.

transitional housing

A type of shelter that provides limited but long-term housing to homeless people with the goal of transitioning them into more permanent homes.

veteran

A person who has served in the military.

ADDITIONAL RESOURCES

SELECTED BIBLIOGRAPHY

Baumohl, Jim, ed. *Homelessness in America.* Phoenix, AZ: The Oryx Press, 1996. Print.

Blau, Joel. *The Visible Poor: Homelessness in the United States.* New York: Oxford UP, 1992. Print.

Hopper, Kim. *Homelessness.* New York: Cornell UP, 2003. Print.

Kozol, Jonathan. *Rachel and Her Children.* New York: Crown Publishers, 1988. Print.

FURTHER READINGS

Hubbard, Jim. *Lives Turned Upside Down: Homeless Children in Their Own Words and Photographs.* New York: Aladdin, 2007. Print.

Kaye, Cathryn Berger. *A Kids' Guide to Hunger & Homelessness: How to Take Action!* Minneapolis, MN: Free Spirit, 2007. Print.

Lopez, Steve. *The Soloist: A Lost Dream, an Unlikely Friendship, and the Redemptive Power of Music.* New York: Penguin, 2008. Print.

Merino, Noel. *Poverty and Homelessness.* Farmington Hills, MI: Greenhaven, 2009. Print.

Web Links

To learn more about homelessness, visit ABDO Publishing Company online at **www.abdopublishing.com**. Web sites about homelessness are featured on our Book Links page. These links are routinely monitored and updated to provide the most current information available.

For More Information

For more information on this subject, contact or visit the following organizations.

National Law Center on Homelessness and Poverty
1411 K Street NW, Suite 1400
Washington, DC 20005
202-638-2535
www.nlchp.org
This organization provides information about homelessness and the law through a newsletter and articles.

The Salvation Army
615 Slaters Lane
Alexandria, VA 22313
800-728-7825
www.salvationarmyusa.org
This organization provides shelter and food programs to people who are homeless. It can also be a resource for those interested in donating food or clothes or volunteering time.

School on Wheels
83 S. Palm
Ventura, CA 93001
805-641-1678
www.schoolonwheels.org
This organization provides tutoring and educational services for children and teens who are homeless.

Source Notes

Chapter 1. Life On the Streets
1. "Getting Homeless Kids Off the Streets through Outreach: Joey's Story." *Covenanthouse.org*. Covenant House, n.d. Web. 1 Feb. 2011.
2. "Homelessness and Poverty in America." *NLCHP.com*. National Law Center on Homelessness and Poverty, 2010. Web. 1 Feb. 2011.
3. America's Youngest Outcasts: State Report Card on Child Homelessness. *Homelesschildrenamerica.org*. National Center on Family Homelessness, 2009. Web. 16 Feb. 2011.
4. Jonathan Kozol. *Rachel and Her Children*. New York: Crown, 1988. Print. 30.
5. Ibid. 3.

Chapter 2. Early Responses to Homelessness
1. Kim Hopper. *Homelessness*. New York: Cornell UP, 2003. Print. 29.
2. Ibid. 30.

Chapter 3. Contemporary Homelessness
1. Joel Blau. *The Visible Poor: Homelessness in the United States*. New York: Oxford UP, 1992. Print. 52.
2. Jim Baumohl, ed. *Homelessness in America*. Phoenix, AZ: The Oryx Press, 1996. Print. 163.
3. Joel Blau. *The Visible Poor: Homelessness in the United States*. New York: Oxford UP, 1992. Print.

Chapter 4. What Does It Mean to Be Homeless?
1. Kim Hopper. *Homelessness*. New York: Cornell UP, 2003. Print. 64.
2. Ibid. 62.
3. Kim Hopper. *Homelessness*. New York: Cornell UP, 2003. Print. 136.
4. "Federal Definition of Homeless." *HUD.gov*. US Department of Housing and Urban Development, n.d. Web. 1 Feb. 2011.
5. Jim Baumohl, ed. *Homelessness in America*. Phoenix, AZ: The Oryx Press, 1996. Print. 3.
6. Rae Bridgman. *Safe Haven: The Story of a Shelter for Homeless Women*. Toronto: U of Toronto P, 2003. Print. 33.

Chapter 5. Who Is Homeless In America?

1. "The Struggle Continues: Homeless Veterans on the Rise." *Veteran Journal*. 25 Oct. 2010. Web. 1 Feb. 2011.

2. US Department of Housing and Urban Development Office of Community Planning and Development. *The 2009 Annual Homeless Assessment Report*. 18 June 2010. Web. 11 Feb. 2011. iii.

3. Joel Blau. *The Visible Poor: Homelessness in the United States*. New York: Oxford UP, 1992. Print. 10.

4. US Department of Housing and Urban Development Office of Community Planning and Development. *The 2009 Annual Homeless Assessment Report*. 18 June 2010. Web. 11 Feb. 2011. 53.

Chapter 6. Causes of Homelessness

1. Jonathan Kozol. *Rachel and Her Children*. New York: Crown, 1988. Print. 57.

2. Kelly Robinson. "A Call Away (From a Place to Stay)." *Hear My Story*. Hear My Story, 1 July 2009. Web. 18 Mar. 2011.

3. Jim Baumohl, ed. *Homelessness in America*. Phoenix, AZ: The Oryx Press, 1996. Print. 25.

4. Ibid.

5. "Affordable Housing." *HUD.gov*. US Department of Housing and Urban Development, n.d. Web. 2 Feb. 2011.

6. Joel Blau. *The Visible Poor: Homelessness in the United States*. New York: Oxford UP, 1992. Print. 45.

Chapter 7. Homelessness and Health

1. Joel Blau. *The Visible Poor: Homelessness in the United States*. New York: Oxford UP, 1992. Print. 26.

2. "Health Care for the Homeless Changed Our Lives." *HCMD. org*. Healthcare for the Homeless, n.d. Web. 2 Feb. 2011.

3. Joel Blau. *The Visible Poor: Homelessness in the United States*. New York: Oxford UP, 1992. Print. 78.

4. Christopher Jencks. *The Homeless*. Cambridge, MA: Harvard UP, 1995. Print. 43.

5. "Dual Diagnosis and Integrated Treatment of Mental Illness and Substance Abuse Disorder." *NAMI.org*. National Alliance on Mental Illness, n.d. Web. 2 Feb. 2011.

Source Notes Continued

Chapter 8. Seeking Shelter

1. "Do Not Handcuff the Poor and Homeless: A Report by the U.S. National Law Center on Homelessness & Poverty and the US National Coalition for the Homeless." *City Mayors Society*. City Mayors Society, 17 July 2009. Web. 1 Feb. 2011.

2. US Department of Housing and Urban Development Office of Community Planning and Development. *The 2009 Annual Homeless Assessment Report*. 18 June 2010. Web. 11 Feb. 2011. 68.

3. Robert Channick. "Suburban Homeless Population Grows; Shelter Crunch Worsens." *Chicago Tribune*, 4 Dec. 2009. Web. 1 Feb. 2011.

4. Sam Allen and Sam Quinones. "Union Rescue Mission to Charge for Some Beds." *Los Angeles Times*, 21 Aug. 2010. Web. 1 Feb. 2011.

5. Carol Morello. "About 44 Million in U.S. Lived Below Poverty Line in 2009, Census Data Show." *Washington Post*, 16 Sept. 2010. Web. 1 Feb. 2011.

Chapter 9. Solutions and Prevention

1. Jim Baumohl, ed. *Homelessness in America*. Phoenix, AZ: The Oryx Press, 1996. Print. 149.

2. Jonathan Kozol. *Rachel and Her Children*. New York: Crown, 1988. Print. 78.

3. Joel Blau. *The Visible Poor: Homelessness in the United States*. New York: Oxford UP, 1992. Print. 109.

4. Jim Baumohl, ed. *Homelessness in America*. Phoenix, AZ: The Oryx Press, 1996. Print. 172.

5. Robert Channick. "Suburban Homeless Population Grows; Shelter Crunch Worsens." *Chicago Tribune*, 4 Dec. 2009. Web. 11 Feb. 2011.

6. Joan Curtain. Personal interview. Nov. 2010.

INDEX

INDEX CONTINUED

ABOUT THE AUTHOR

A. M. Buckley is an artist, writer, and children's book author based in Los Angeles, California. A former elementary school teacher, she has written several books for children, including *The Kids' Yoga Deck*. In high school, Buckley had an opportunity to volunteer at a homeless shelter. This experience led her to become a regular volunteer for a homeless service group as a student at the University of California in Berkeley. She continues the practice today, volunteering with an organization aiding the homeless population of Hollywood.

PHOTO CREDITS

Dennie Cody/Getty Images, cover, 3; Mike Calamungi/AP Images, 6; Dean Humphrey/AP Images, 11; Shehzad Noorani/ AP Images, 15; Alice Barber Stephens/Library of Congress, 16, 96 (top); American Stock Archive/Getty Images, 19, 97 (left); AP Images, 23, 97 (right); Lennox McLendon/AP Images, 24; Spencer Platt/ Getty Images, 28; Kristen Wyatt/AP Images, 33; Alan Diaz/ AP Images, 34; Remy de la Mauviniere/AP Images, 38; Melanie Stetson Freeman/Getty Images, 43; Mel Evans/AP Images, 44, 75; Red Line Editorial, 51, 59; Eric Risberg/AP Images, 53; Bebeto Matthews/AP Images, 54; Bloomberg/Getty Images, 65; Lacy Atkins/AP Images, 66; Charles Krupa/AP Images, 69, 96 (bottom); Bonile Bam/Getty Images, 76, 98 (top); John Gress/ Getty Images, 79, 98 (bottom); Robert Nickelsberg/Getty Images, 83, 99 (right); Mark Ralston/Getty Images, 84, 95; Leigh Vogel/ Getty Images, 91

D1607383